Learning to Read, Step by Step!

Ready to Read   Preschool–Kindergarten
• big type and easy words • rhyme and rhythm • picture clues
For children who know the alphabet and are eager to begin reading.

Reading with Help   Preschool–Grade 1
• basic vocabulary • short sentences • simple stories
For children who recognize familiar words and sound out new words with help.

Reading on Your Own   Grades 1–3
• engaging characters • easy-to-follow plots • popular topics
For children who are ready to read on their own.

Reading Paragraphs   Grades 2–3
• challenging vocabulary • short paragraphs • exciting stories
For newly independent readers who read simple sentences with confidence.

Ready for Chapters   Grades 2–4
• chapters • longer paragraphs • full-color art
For children who want to take the plunge into chapter books but still like colorful pictures.

STEP INTO READING® is designed to give every child a successful reading experience. The grade levels are only guides; children will progress through the steps at their own speed, developing confidence in their reading. The F&P Text Level on the back cover serves as another tool to help you choose the right book for your child.

Remember, a lifetime love of reading starts with a single step!

To Michael Scott Fritz —J.F.

To my wife, Cynthia —C.R.

Text copyright © 1993 by Jean Fritz
Cover art and interior illustrations copyright © 1993 by Charles Robinson

Map on p. 4 by Kathryn Klanderman

Photograph credits: pp. 9, 13, 15, 21, The Lincoln Museum, Fort Wayne, Indiana, a part of Lincoln National Corporation.

Visit us on the Web!
StepIntoReading.com
rhcbooks.com

Educators and librarians, for a variety of teaching tools, visit us at
RHTeachersLibrarians.com

Library of Congress Cataloging-in-Publication Data is available upon request.
ISBN 978-0-593-43278-5 (trade) — ISBN 978-0-593-43279-2 (lib. bdg.)

Printed in the United States of America
10 9 8 7 6 5 4 3 2 1

This book has been officially leveled by using the F&P Text Level Gradient™ Leveling System.

STEP INTO READING®

4 STEP READING PARAGRAPHS

A HISTORY READER

Just a Few Words, Mr. Lincoln

The Story of the Gettysburg Address

by Jean Fritz

illustrations by Charles Robinson

Random House 🏠 New York

AMERICA DURING THE CIVIL WAR

Gettysburg, Pennsylvania

Washington, D.C.

N
W   E
S

Northern States

Southern States

President Lincoln was one busy man.

He had two big jobs.

He had to free the slaves.

And he had to win the war. The Civil War. It had begun in 1861—Americans against Americans. Some southern states had quit the Union. They wanted their own country, they said.

But Lincoln couldn't let them run off like that. This was the *United* States, wasn't it? That's the way it had started. That's the way it should be.

Besides these big jobs, the president had little jobs, too. He had to shake hands.

Everyone wanted to shake the president's hand. So he shook and shook and shook. Often his own hand was swollen afterward.

And he had to write letters. From all over the country, people wrote to him. Why didn't he do this? Why hadn't he done that? Some just wanted his autograph. He couldn't take time to write "Abraham Lincoln." So he just wrote "A. Lincoln."

"Dear Sir
You request an
autograph, and here it is
                    Yours truly
                    A. Lincoln"

People even lined up outside his office to see him. They buzzed around his door like bees, he said. All had hard-luck stories. When he could, the president helped them. He hated to say no.

But sometimes there was a special knock on his door. Three light taps and two loud thumps. This wasn't a hard-luck story. This was the president's ten-year-old son, Tad. His real name was Thomas, but his nickname was Tad. Why? He was just like a tadpole, his father said. Wriggly.

Abraham and Tad Lincoln

Tad and his father were best friends. Sometimes they played and roughhoused together before supper.

Sometimes Tad went with his father to visit the soldiers. He'd wear his own uniform, carry his own sword, and ride his own little gray horse. Sometimes he'd walk with his father to the War Department for the latest news.

Tad in his uniform

Tad drew a mustache on his picture so he'd look like a real general.

Often the news was bad. For the first two years of the war, everything went wrong.

The soldiers needed blankets. But the blankets they got turned out to be rotten.

They needed knapsacks. The knapsacks fell apart.

Worst of all, the South kept winning. Battle after battle. Lincoln said his generals had the "slows." They didn't move fast enough. Or hard enough. Or soon enough.

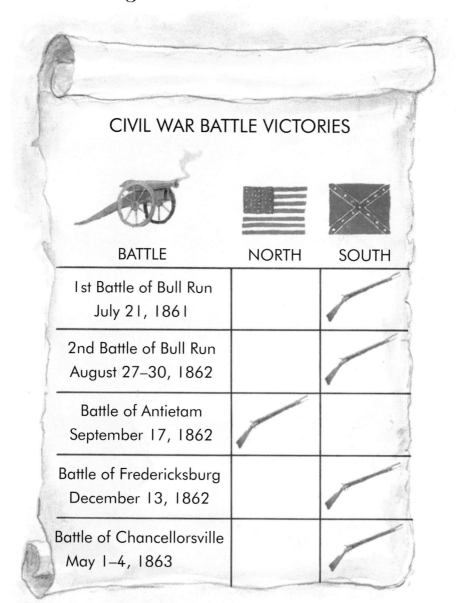

CIVIL WAR BATTLE VICTORIES

BATTLE	NORTH	SOUTH
1st Battle of Bull Run July 21, 1861		🔫
2nd Battle of Bull Run August 27–30, 1862		🔫
Battle of Antietam September 17, 1862	🔫	
Battle of Fredericksburg December 13, 1862		🔫
Battle of Chancellorsville May 1–4, 1863		🔫

Then, in July 1863, the southern army moved north. They were going to whip the Yankees on their own land. So they marched into Pennsylvania.

Near the little town of Gettysburg, the two armies met. And fought. For three days cannons boomed. Swords flashed. Horses reared and screamed. It was a terrible battle. Twenty thousand southern soldiers were killed or wounded. Twenty-three thousand northern ones.

The North won. Lincoln was thankful. Still, he felt sad. So many dead boys! Not one of them ready to die. And the war wasn't even over. "My heart is like lead," he said.

People decided to build a special cemetery in Gettysburg. Just for the fallen soldiers. And they would hold a special service to honor them. They set the date for October 23. And they asked Edward Everett to speak. He was the grandest speaker in the country. He looked grand. He rolled out grand words in a grand way.

But Mr. Everett needed more time to put his grand words together. So the date was changed to November 19. Then the people thought: The president should speak, too. Not long. Just a few words, they said.

Edward Everett

President Lincoln did have something to say. But he'd keep his speech short, he said. "Short, short, short." He wanted to talk about why they were fighting. Not just to win. Not just to free the slaves. But to keep America the way George Washington had meant it to be. A country run *by* the people. *For* the people. *All* the people. United. With no hard feelings when the war was over.

He wanted his speech to be just right. But, of course, President Lincoln was one busy man. Still, by November 15 his speech was almost done. He'd even read it aloud to see how the words sounded. All it needed was "another lick," he said.

Tad wasn't around while his father was writing. He was in bed. Sick. The doctor didn't know what was wrong. That was not a good sign, Mrs. Lincoln said. She was beside herself with worry. The president was, too. He just hoped Tad would be better before he went to Gettysburg.

On November 18, Lincoln had to leave. And Tad was not better. His fever was still high. Of course Tad had to take medicine, but he didn't like it. Sometimes only his father could get him to take it. And his father was leaving. It was hard for Lincoln to say good-bye. But he had to.

Lincoln went to Gettysburg in a special four-car train. It was decorated with red, white, and blue streamers. And it was filled with important people. All of them wanted to talk with the president.

So the president talked. All the way to Gettysburg. The story is told that Lincoln wrote his speech on the train. Just scratched it out on the back of an old envelope. That is not true. His speech was in his pocket—all written except for a last "lick."

In Gettysburg everyone wanted to honor the president. That evening a group of singers sang to him and then asked for a speech. But the president told them he had nothing to say. If he tried, he might say something foolish. The singers didn't think much of that. They just hoped the president would do better the next day.

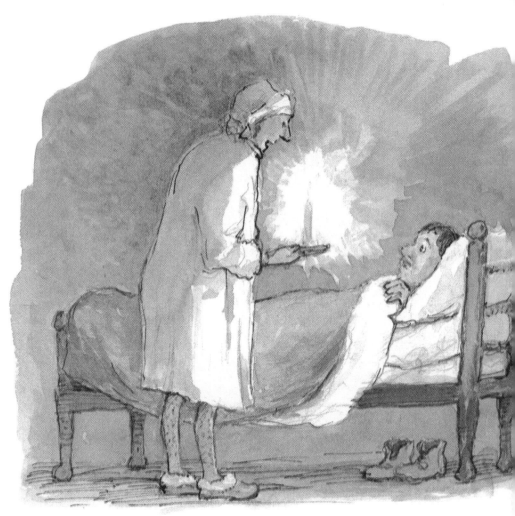

Gettysburg was crowded with visitors.
Important visitors. In the house where
Lincoln was staying, there were not even
enough beds to go around. Mr. Everett
was told he might have to share his bed
with the governor. But at the last minute
another bed was found for the governor.

Mr. Everett's daughter was not so lucky. She had to share her bed with two other ladies. It was too much for the bed. It broke down in the middle of the night. The three ladies crashed to the floor.

President Lincoln, of course, had a room to himself. But before going to bed, he went over his speech. He gave it a last lick. Yet he kept thinking about Tad. How was he? Had his fever gone down? Luckily, a telegram arrived from Mrs. Lincoln. Tad was much better, she said. That was just what Lincoln wanted to hear. He had never read sweeter-sounding words.

November 19 was a bright, sunny day. At ten o'clock in the morning, Lincoln went outside. A horse was waiting for him. A short horse. And Lincoln was a tall man. Six-feet-four, with long legs.

People laughed about how long the president's legs were. But they seemed about right to him, he said. Just long enough to reach the ground. But that day, with a horse between his legs, they still almost reached the ground.

For the big parade to the cemetery, the president was given a bigger horse. A big, proud-looking chestnut horse. No one could miss Lincoln now. There he is! people said. See? In his high stovepipe hat!

First came the band. Then soldiers. Then President Lincoln, some state governors, and other important people. But not Mr. Everett. He had gone to see the battlefield, and he wasn't back.

At the cemetery the president climbed on the platform. A small sofa was there for him. But out in front the people had to stand. Fifteen to twenty thousand of them. Crowding close. Jostling each other. Fathers holding children on their shoulders. All trying to see the president.

Mr. Everett was to speak first. But he still had not come. So everyone waited. The band played, and the people stood. And the president sat, looking out at the fields. At all the fresh graves. And wooden markers. Thousands of wooden markers. And under every marker was the body of a fallen soldier.

At last Mr. Everett came. Of course he was worth waiting for. Just listen to that voice! people said. Making a grand story of the Battle of Gettysburg. Placing it right beside the great battles of history.

But he didn't stop. For one solid hour he talked. People expected Mr. Everett to talk a long time. They loved what he said. Still, they were standing. They were tired. And hungry. For another hour Mr. Everett talked.

Then a glee club sang.

Then—at last!

The President of the United States!

President Lincoln stood, put on a pair of steel-rimmed spectacles, and pulled a single sheet of paper from his pocket.

Lincoln talked as if he were talking to every single person in the country. Telling them not to give up on the idea of one country. He talked as if he were talking to George Washington, too. Telling him that they wouldn't let him down. And as if he were talking to the fallen soldiers. Telling them they had not died for nothing.

It was a short speech, and it was over. Ten sentences, 271 words. Lincoln sat down.

People were so excited to hear the president, they had hardly begun to listen to what he said. They were still noticing his accent. He had a Kentucky accent. After all this time! But suddenly there he was—sitting down! He was finished. It took longer to boil an egg.

They clapped, but perhaps they
were slow about it. In any case, Lincoln
supposed his speech had fizzled. It "fell
like a wet blanket," he said. He was sure
that no one would remember what was
said here. He'd even said so in his speech.

All afternoon Lincoln shook hands with the people of Gettysburg. When he got on the train that evening, he was tired. He put his long legs up on a train seat. And he closed his eyes. He had no idea that his speech would be printed in newspapers all over the country. And that people would read it. Again and again. And praise it.

Even Mr. Everett wrote to Lincoln. The president had said more in two minutes, Mr. Everett declared, than he had said in two hours. Americans agreed. They would remember Lincoln's words and go on remembering. It was one of the greatest speeches in American history.

But by the time Lincoln heard what was being said, he was doing other things.

After all, he was one busy man.

This is the speech President Lincoln gave at Gettysburg:

Four score and seven years ago our fathers brought forth on this continent, a new nation, conceived in Liberty, and dedicated to the proposition that all men are created equal.

Now we are engaged in a great civil war, testing whether that nation, or any nation so conceived and so dedicated, can long endure. We are met on a great battlefield of that war. We have come to dedicate a portion of that field, as a final resting place for those who here gave their lives that that nation might live. It is altogether fitting and proper that we should do this.

But, in a larger sense, we can not dedicate—we can not consecrate—we can not hallow—this ground. The brave men, living and dead, who struggled here, have consecrated it, far above our poor power to add or detract. The world will little note, nor long remember what we say here, but it can never forget what they did here. It is for us the living, rather, to be dedicated here to the unfinished work which they who fought here have thus far so nobly advanced. It is rather for us to be here dedicated to the great task remaining before us—that from these honored dead we take increased devotion to that cause for which they gave the last full measure of devotion—that we here highly resolve that these dead shall not have died in vain—that this nation, under God, shall have a new birth of freedom—and that government of the people, by the people, for the people, shall not perish from the earth.